OH, NO! MORE CANADIANS!

Hysterically Historical Rhymes

GORDON SNELL

With caricatures by
AISLIN

McArthur & Company
Toronto

FIRST PRINTING

Canadian Cataloguing in Publication Data

Snell, Gordon
Oh, no! more Canadians!: hysterically historical rhymes

ISBN 1–55278–002–3

1. Celebrities – Canada – Poetry. 2. Humourous poetry, English.
3. Canadian wit and humour, Pictorial. I. Aislin. II. Title.

PR6069.N44054 1998   821′.914   C98–931679–3

Cover Illustration by *AISLIN*
Layout, Design and Electronic Imaging by *MARY HUGHSON*
Printed and Bound in Canada by
TRANSCONTINENTAL PRINTING, TORONTO

McArthur & Company

Toronto
322 KING STREET WEST, SUITE 402, TORONTO,
ONTARIO, CANADA, M5V 1J2

To Maeve, who makes me so elated,
These rhymes with love are dedicated.

GS

These cartoons of oddballs,
Eccentrics and sorts,
Are dedicated to Mary,
And a life of loose shorts

A

OH, NO! MORE CANADIANS!

Hysterically Historical Rhymes

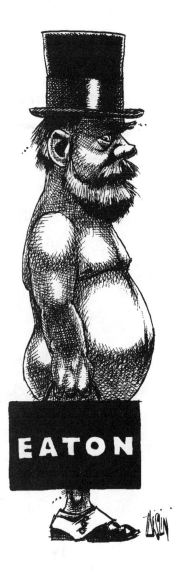

Contents

SAMUEL DE CHAMPLAIN
(1570-1635)

(Samuel de Champlain was an enthusiastic explorer and map-maker who founded France's first colony in the New World at Quebec in 1608.)

Champlain was eager to advance
His country's glory, in New France.
The best maps of the region then,
Came from his cartographic pen.
From Port-Royal, his earliest post,
He mapped the whole New England coast.

Explorers' trips, he realized,
Were best if locally advised.
So he made friendships, for insurance,
With the Algonquins and the Hurons.
When with these tribes his friendship grew
He travelled with them by canoe
And that was how he came to know
Lakes Huron and Ontario.
Then at another lake, said he:
"Let's call it Champlain, after me !"

Samuel was brave - among his stunts,
He shot the rapids, more than once.

Champlain was able to persuade
The French King that enormous trade
Would flow, if colonies were made.

He even thought it would be cute
When someone found the China route
To have on the Atlantic coast
A lucrative French Customs post.

After much thought, he chose the lands
Just in the place Quebec now stands.
His plans at first went topsy-turvy
When many settlers died of scurvy,
But Champlain never had a doubt:
He grew wheat, made a pool for trout,
And had a grand town plan laid out.

To make the winters seem less drear
He formed the Order of Good Cheer.
They'd hunt game for the festive table
And drink as much as they were able.

In transatlantic sailing ships
Champlain made over twenty trips,
And after one, he would decide:
"I'm forty - time I took a bride!"
The records, though, have never told
Just why he chose one, twelve years old.

Nor why, despite a happy life
In due course, with his grown-up wife,
He chose at last his will to vary
And leave all to the Virgin Mary.

He was exceedingly devout
And brought religious orders out
Among the tribes to make excursions
Attempting to promote conversions.

His colony survived a check -
The English capture of Quebec.
But then another deal was done:
Champlain was back, as Number One.
If thwarted, he cried: "Sacre Bleu! -
I'm here to act for Richelieu!"

He died, to solemn lamentation,
Where his first humble habitation
Had founded the Canadian nation.

ROBERT CAVELIER DE LA SALLE
(1643-1687)

(La Salle crossed the Atlantic to New France
with an ambition to explore and to grow rich. He
achieved these aims, but not entirely successfully,
since he both found - and lost - the Mississippi.)

La Salle, a would-be Jesuit,
After nine years was asked to quit.
Sulking, he said: "I'll take a chance
And try my fortune in New France."

A man devoid of inhibition,
He joined up with an expedition,
Telling the leaders: "I'm your boy,
For I speak fluent Iroquois."

His claim was shown to be absurd -
He couldn't understand a word.
But he declared: "I'll soon be back!"
And Governor General Frontenac
To whom he showed extreme servility
Promoted him to the nobility.

Back home in France, at Court he schemed
To clinch the deal of which he dreamed,
And soon two clerics with ambition
Helped get La Salle an expedition.
Then joyfully he shouted: "Yipee!
I'll sail right down the Mississippi!"

And so La Salle went sailing south
Right down the river to its mouth.
He then dressed up, so we are told,
In robes of scarlet and of gold
And stated: "I did everything
For Louis, France's glorious King.
He's now the Lord of this Nirvana -
Let's call the place LOUISIANA!"

The fur trade made his fortune grow;
His fort on Lake Ontario
And other ventures made La Salle
A V.I.P. in *Montréal.*

Then being a devious sort of chap
He showed the King a bogus map
Charting the Mississippi's flow
Far west of where it ought to go.
He told the King: "With this, it's true,
We'll conquer Mexico for you!"

He meant to land as he intended,
Just where the Mississippi ended;
But though he'd sailed it all before
He couldn't find it any more.
He told his party: "I'm afraid
The Mississippi's been mislaid!"

So up and down the coast they sailed
To seek the Delta, but they failed.

Sensing his men were in a tizz
La Salle said smoothly: "Here it is!"

They said: "This guy begins to vex us -
This, clearly, is the coast of Texas.
And we're so weary and sick of trying,
And while you're living, you'll go on lying -
Your Old Man River may disappear
But your own end is getting near.
Your fortunes now have reached rock bottom."
With that, they stood him up and shot him.

Considering La Salle's behaviour,
His claims to be their guide and saviour,
His grasping greed and his cupidity,
His treachery and sheer stupidity,
We all might wonder more and more
Just why he wasn't killed before!

LAURA SECORD
(1775-1868)

(In the War of 1812, Laura Secord made an epic solo trek to warn the troops at Beaver Dams of a coming attack. Public recognition and reward were a long time coming, but she finally got her deserved fame, as well as her name on monuments and chocolate boxes.)

In history, the name of Laura
Has come to have a certain aura,
Although it's true that no one now
Remembers what they called her cow.

In 1812 the Yankees, sore
At Canada, began a war.
The Secords, on the British side,
Found that their home was occupied.
The U.S. officers with pride,
Declaring they would soon be winners,
Told Laura she must cook their dinners.

What could she do? There in her house
She watched the officers carouse.
She listened too, as they began
To boast about their battle plan.
They said, "These troops of Uncle Sam's
Will wipe them out at Beaver Dams!"

So Laura thought, "I must give warning!"
Before the sun rose in the morning

She slipped away, quite undetected,
To say attack should be expected.

The day dawned and the hot sun shone
But Laura just walked on and on
Through undergrowth and hidden by-ways
Avoiding checkpoints, roads and highways.

She waded many a stream and river
Her urgent message to deliver,
And found her courage sorely tested
In treacherous swamps, by snakes infested.
And some accounts will tell you how
By clinging to a passing cow
She managed with this bovine aid
The soldiers' capture to evade.

She reached Niagara, and she paled:
How could that craggy cliff be scaled?
But Laura's courage never failed.
She climbed and clung and didn't stop
Until she'd reached the very top.

With darkness falling all around her,
A group of Mohawk warriors found her.
With wonder and concern they scanned her,
And brought her to the post's commander.

"Well, you deserve," said James FitzGibbon,
"A campaign medal and a ribbon.

I'll send the Mohawks on their track
And mount a great surprise attack!"

His victory hopes were not mistaken -
Five hundred prisoners were taken;
And everyone admired the way
That Laura Secord saved the day.

In spite of her courageous mission
Poor Laura got no recognition.
She sent out many a petition
In which she always chanced to mention
It would be nice to get a pension.

When more than forty years had passed
Her deed was recognized at last.
The Prince of Wales, the future King,
Just happened to be visiting
And made, among his many calls,
A visit to Niagara Falls.

Here it was brought to his attention
That Laura merited a pension.
He sent one hundred pounds all told;
Laura, now eighty-six years old,
Declared: "Well, better late than never!
At least my name will live for ever."

And when she died, her name was praised
And several monuments were raised.

In 1913, Frank O'Connor
Said, "Laura's name I'd like to honour.
She lived life well, and took the knocks -
I'll put her on my chocolate box!
Her portrait will be fine and dandy
Paraded on my luscious candy."

So Laura's name has never perished
Wherever chocolate is cherished.

DR. JAMES BARRY
(1795-1865)

(James Barry was an army surgeon who rose to high rank and was put in charge of all Canada's military hospitals. When he died it was discovered that Dr. Barry was a woman.)

No woman could be asked to marry
The famous surgeon called James Barry.
He'd have to stay upon the shelf,
For he was that same sex himself.

She played a man not from perversity,
But just to get to university.
In Edinburgh she - or he -
Obtained a medical degree.
Then she began within a year
An army medical career.

And soon she thought, "What I deserve is
A spell in the Colonial Service."
So her career began to burgeon
In Cape Town, as Assistant Surgeon,
And once when typhus there was rife
She even saved the Governor's life.

Her temper, though, was quite a scandal -
She often flew right off the handle.
Her macho image she would fuel
Sometimes, by fighting in a duel.

Her ghost, the Cape Town legends say,
Still haunts a glen beside a bay.

Her brilliance was duly noted
And she was constantly promoted.
She reached the height of army fame
When out to Canada she came.
The hospitals both small and large
Were all in Dr. Barry's charge.
In army ranks she caused some storms
By pushing through a few reforms.

"Separate quarters," said James Barry,
"Should be the right of men who marry -
And what is more, the soldiers' diet
Is dull enough to cause disquiet.
They'll find a roast a great relief
From eating nothing but boiled beef.

Now, those straw pillows on each bed -
Put feathers in them all instead.
Water and drains too, need improving.
Well, don't just stand and stare - get moving!"

The thankful soldiers soon began
To say, "James Barry - he's our man!"

The doctor relished ostentation -
In fact she caused a great sensation:
Through Montreal she made her way

In fur coat, in a scarlet sleigh,
A black manservant at her side
With a small dog, her pet and pride.

The secret she had kept concealed,
After her death was soon revealed.
The powers-that-be made quite a fuss -
They cried, "She made a fool of us!
A woman surgeon, in the army -
The very notion drives us barmy!"

Such things were quite beyond their ken:
She'd taken on the world of men
And shown, the only way she could,
That women could be just as good.
She really opened up their eyes,
This feminist, in male disguise.

SAMUEL CUNARD
(1787 - 1865)

(Born and brought up in Halifax, Nova Scotia, Samuel Cunard joined his father's shipping company and pioneered the use of steamships on the transatlantic route. The Cunard Line grew to be one of the most prestigious operators of liners, famous for their speed, luxury and reliability.)

A boy in Halifax would stay
Upon the docks and gaze all day
At sailing ships of every sort
Coming and going in the port.
Samuel Cunard had dreams that he
Would own a shipping company.

His father, a carpenter, saved hard
And bought a mail-boat - soon Cunard
Became indeed a noted name
Destined for even greater fame.

One day in England, Sam was on
The steam train built by Stephenson.
He came home with a novel notion:
Steam could take ships across the ocean!

In Boston, where he looked for cash,
The merchants said, "It's much too rash.
Such foolish schemes are sure to fail,
For Steam will never conquer Sail."

The British though were not so nervous:
They planned a transatlantic service
To carry mail by using steam,
And so they welcomed Samuel's scheme.

Britannia was Cunard's first ship
To make the transatlantic trip.
Sixty-three passengers set sail
As well as copious bags of mail.
Samuel Cunard was there on board
To hear the dockside crowds who roared.
The Captain shouted orders through
A speaking trumpet to the crew.
The steam the engines would provide
Drove giant paddles, either side.

Among the crew there were three cats
To deal with mailbag-eating rats.
A cow too in a padded stall
Would yield fresh milk for one and all.
The passengers at meals might dine
On pea soup, fish pie, meat and wine,
And breakfast could be steak with hock,
For drinks were served from six o'clock.

When the ship rolled, the sea would slosh
Downstairs, and make the rooms awash.
For sea-sick people, stewards kept handy
Glasses of water mixed with brandy.

But in twelve days Britannia came
To Halifax, with great acclaim.
And on to Boston then she sailed
Where as a hero Sam was hailed.
With banquets and a big parade
Great tribute to Cunard was paid.
Soon he was undisputed king
Of transatlantic travelling.

The Admiralty then made a move
Of which Cunard did not approve.
His ships were requisitioned for
The troops of the Crimean War,
And many journeys then they made
With horses for the Light Brigade.

And wounded soldiers too were brought
Across the Black Sea to the port
Where skillful nursing was provided,
And Florence Nightingale presided.

After the War, the north Atlantic
Saw other battles no less frantic,
For U.S. lines were fighting hard
To wrest the laurels from Cunard.

The Collins Line pulled out all stops
With private bathrooms, barber shops,
Deep carpets and electric bells
And brass spittoons too, shaped like shells.

Cunard's speed records they must beat
To make their victory complete.
The Collins Line achieved success
By crossing in ten days or less.

Cunard competed to eclipse
Its rivals with new, bigger ships -
But Samuel always stressed the need
To favour safety over speed.

The Collins Line, which took more chances,
Wrecked ships, and wrecked its own finances.
Eventually the Line was gone,
But sturdily Cunard sailed on.

Sam died in 1865;
His liners kept his name alive.
Cunard's esteem would never vary:
The Queens, Elizabeth and Mary,
The QE2, Cunard Princess,
Continued to ensure success.

And all that power and esteem
Came from young Samuel's boyhood dream
Watching the ships sail to and fro
In Halifax, so long ago.

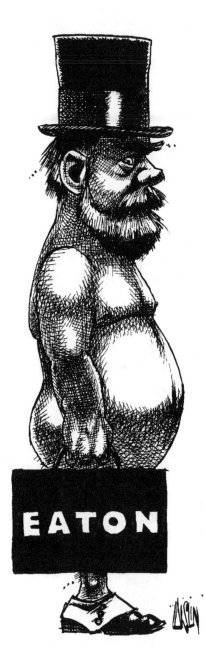

TIMOTHY EATON
(1834-1907)

*(Timothy Eaton founded the first of the Eaton chain of stores in
Toronto in 1869, and his commercial ideas revolutionized shopping
in Canada.)*

From Ireland to Canadian shores
To found a famous chain of stores
Came Timothy Eaton, now renowned
Wherever shoppers can be found.

Shopping was ripe for revolution
And Eaton had his own solution;
And so in 1869
The first store in the Eaton line
At Yonge Street started operation
And caused at once a big sensation.

Eaton began with great panache,
Declaring: "We take only cash.
The barter system, we have shed it -
What's more, you needn't ask for credit,
Because you just ain't gonna geddit!

Don't seek to bargain, for we won't -
You pay our fixed price, or you don't.
We offer value and fair play -
That's retailing, the Eaton way!"

But one more promise Eaton made
Really amazed the retail trade:
He said, "We'll give back what you paid
If you are not quite satisfied
With any product we supplied."

His rivals scoffed, and said disaster
Would come within a year, or faster.
But Timothy soon proved them wrong
As shoppers to his store did throng.

And what was even more surprising,
He wanted honest advertising -
Insisting, "Everything must be
Exactly what we guarantee.
No lies and no exaggeration
Must mar the Eaton reputation."

He made more innovations later -
Even installed an elevator.
When customers at first were wary
He tried to show it wasn't scary:
Wax figures then were put inside
And up and down were seen to ride -
A ruse that was a bit surprising
From one who liked true advertising.

Now as the Eaton empire grew
He pioneered mail-order too.
His catalogue was justly famed:

The Prairie Bible it was named.

While Eaton's name grew more prestigious
The founder still remained religious.
He hated liquor, wouldn't let
His stores sell any cigarette.
At home, nobody had the chance
To play a game of cards, or dance.

At work, he was paternalist -
A fervent anti-unionist.
His workers even were afraid
To watch the Labour Day parade.

And yet, unlike the rest, he'd fix
For Eaton's stores to close at six;
And afternoons on Saturday
He said should be a holiday.

His methods prospered - soon he'd boast
A chain of stores from coast to coast.
Then, with the founding father gone,
His sons and grandsons carried on.

SAMUEL STEELE
(1849 - 1919)

(Samuel Steele was one of the first Mounties, and his long career took him west to police the Yukon during the Klondike Gold Rush, when he kept law and order in unruly places like Dawson City.)

Among the very first recruits
To don the Mounties' riding boots
And give the new force such appeal
Was Sergeant Major Samuel Steele.

His troop knew not what lay in store:
They trekked nine hundred miles and more
To keep their pledge and do their best
To police the new lands of the west.

They would establish law and order
Unlike the land across the border
Where guns and greed ruled every town
And soldiers hunted Indians down.
The Mounted Police wore coats of red
In case the natives turned and fled
Thinking they were that force of dread,
The U.S. Cavalry, instead.

For Sam Steele, life was never quiet:
He faced rebellion and riot,
Then in the 1890's came
The Gold Rush Years that made his name.

From way off down the Yukon River
Came rumours that made strong men quiver -
Rumours that would fulfill their dreams:
"It seems there's gold in them thar streams!"

So up towards the Passes then
Climbed thousands of gold-hungry men.
In struggling lines the great Stampede
Moved at a slow, laborious speed.

Many a man bore on his back
Possessions crammed into a pack.
Others dragged sleds, and quite a few
Used horses, dogs and reindeer too.
The leader of one Scottish group
Played bagpipes to inspire his troop.

There at the summit, Steele presided.
No man could pass, unless provided
With food and clothes and other gear
To last him for at least a year.
So, many times, those trudging men
Had to go down and back again
Until with their supplies at last
The Mounties would allow them past.

Frozen, and lashed by icy gales,
Many gave up the Gold Rush trails,
While others found they could not bear
The constant stench that hovered there

Of rotting horse-flesh, in the air.

Diseases claimed their victims too,
But twenty thousand made it through,
And down the Yukon with elation
They sailed towards their destination.

They found no end to their privation,
For Dawson City faced starvation.
Gold was in plentiful supply
But with no food, what could it buy?

The city struggled but survived -
And when snows melted, how it thrived!
Smart restaurants served caviar,
And liquor flowed in every bar.

The dance hall orchestras would play
As miners danced the night away.
While those whose tastes were more demure
Found that church choirs had more allure.

The Klondike Kings, the richest men,
Had fortunes spent, and made again.
Swiftwater Bill was one, so fine
He'd only take a bath in wine.
He paid, or so the story's told,
A Dance Hall girl her weight in gold.
One singer who was all the rage
Found golden nuggets thrown on stage.

The customers quite often paid
In gold dust which the barmen weighed.
These barmen who were deft and slick
Kept their hands damp, so some would stick.

For all the characters around
Apt nicknames could be always found:
Diamond-Tooth Gertie, Lime Juice Lil,
And Two-Step Louie, never still;
While Klondike Kate the dancing led,
A candelabra on her head.

This motley crowd Steele did police:
He made the rules and kept the peace,
Licensed the gambling clubs, objected
If Sunday wasn't well respected.

The Red Light District too obeyed
When told the girls could not parade
Till four p.m. had come and gone -
Then they were free to carry on.

Steele prosecuted as obscene
Comedians who mocked the Queen.
Con-men who did the miners down
He simply banished from the town.
But his attempts to stem corruption
Brought his career an interruption.
A devious, powerful politician
Dismissed him fast from his position.

Though many a protest and petition
From Dawson City's population
Pleaded for Sam Steele's restoration
The Klondike town would hear no more
The Lion of the Yukon's roar.

Though his career would have a score
Of other triumphs still in store,
It took the Yukon to reveal
The towering strength of Samuel Steele.

No wonder that the crowds turned out
To cry farewell, and cheer and shout,
And deemed it was a shameful pity
That Steele was leaving Dawson City.

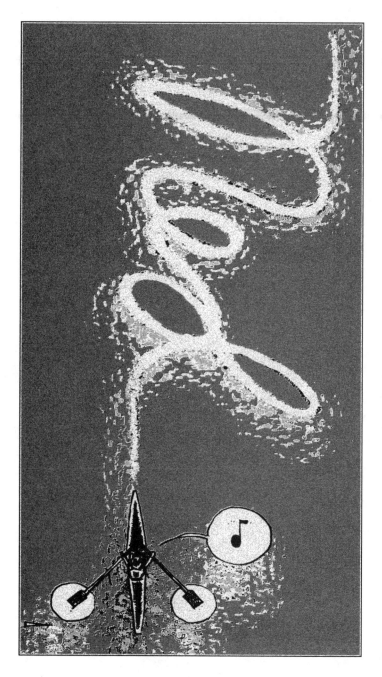

NED HANLAN
(1855-1908)

(Toronto-born Ned Hanlan spent much of his childhood in rowing boats, and became such a superb oarsman that in single sculls races he was five times world champion.)

Upon Toronto Island's shore
Ned Hanlan's father kept a store.
He told the boy, "It is the rule
For kids your age to go to school."
So Ned said, "Since I've got to go there,
The simplest way will be to row there."

For Ned loved rowing in his boat
And spent his boyhood years afloat.
By eighteen, he was doing well:
At single sculls he did excel
And was declared by those who know
The best in all Ontario.

He showed it was no idle claim:
Canadian Champion he became.
Soon after, south he took a trip
And won the U.S. Championship.

And then in England, on Thames' banks
Spectators thronged in peering ranks;
A hundred thousand cheered to see
Ned Hanlan row to victory.

At home, triumphant flags unfurled -
Ned was the Champion of the World!

And his successes then were stunning:
He won the title five years running.
With his moustache and curly hair
Ned was so smooth and debonair,
When he was racing anywhere
Excited crowds would always go
To watch their sporting hero row.
And as they cheered him long and loud,
Ned Hanlan entertained the crowd.
For such a speedy guy was Ned
That he was always way ahead;
So then he paused and smiled and gave
The watching crowds a friendly wave
And did some clowning while he'd stopped,
Pretending that his oars had dropped.

He'd row around in circles too
Until his rivals came in view;
Then as they panted up behind him,
Streaking ahead once more they'd find him.

In making light of his position
Ned followed in a great tradition:
New Brunswick fishermen did score
A big success some years before,
Becoming top World Champion Four.

They used to carry wine to sup
Till their opponents caught them up,
And when they did, then just like Ned,
They'd promptly go full speed ahead.

Although today's Canadian crews
Don't carry with them crates of booze,
In triumph and in dedication
They look to Ned for inspiration.

THE DONNELLYS
(d. 1880)

(The Donnelly family terrorized their local neighborhood in Ontario for over twenty years of robbery, rustling and murder. In 1880 James Carroll led a vigilante group against them, intent on wholesale massacre. . .)

The Donnellys from Tipperary
Had habits that were really scary.
Johannah and her husband James
With ruthless violence made their names.

They and their seven sons would go
Round Lucan in Ontario
Like madmen roaring into battle.
They torched the barns and stole the cattle
And murdered travellers for cash.
Away on horseback they would dash
To revel, laugh and count their plunder.
It really isn't any wonder
That policemen who were posted there
Preferred to seek a job elsewhere.

And thus for over two decades
The feared Black Donnellys made their raids.
But then James Carroll took a hand
And gathered up a vengeful band.

At dead of night, with blade and shot,
They tried to massacre the lot.
Although a few escaped and fled,
Most of the Donnellys were dead.

James Carroll to the court-house went;
Though some who saw that night's event
Described the murders they had spied,
"NOT GUILTY!" all the jury cried.

In spite of facts, there's few who'd say
That justice wasn't done that day.
Most people clearly shared the view
Declared by twelve good men and true.

The murdering Donnellys are gone
And yet their legend lingers on.
Some local people give their word
That ghostly hooves at night are heard.
I can believe it - maybe you can:
The Donnellys still lurk in Lucan!

LOUIS RIEL
(1844-1885)

(Louis Riel led two rebellions trying to establish lands and rights for the Métis, descendants of indigenous peoples and early European settlers. His campaigns both peaceful and military, led to the founding of Manitoba, but his eventual trial and execution caused long-lasting and passionate controversy.)

The Métis, from two races grown,
Became a nation of their own.
To the Red River thousands went
And made a farming settlement,
And twice a year they all would go
To hunt the herds of buffalo.

This bright boy from the distant prairie
Went eastward to a seminary.
In Montreal his education
Earned him a dazzling reputation.
Mastering Math, French, Greek and Latin,
Louis topped every class he sat in.

And while the boy was educated
Four provinces were federated
To make what was, in their opinion,
A most spectacular Dominion.

Sir John Macdonald was Prime Minister.
The Métis didn't think him sinister;
But Canada approached one day

The Company called Hudson's Bay
And told them the Dominion planned
To buy out most of 'Rupert's Land'.
They said, "We fear a confrontation
Will lead to US annexation
Unless it's checked by our new nation."

Although the land was bought and sold
The people living there weren't told.
So when they saw surveyors there
Rebellion was in the air.
Louis, their chosen leader, went
To ask what these intruders meant.
"You have no rights here," said Riel.
(The less polite said, "Go to hell!")

The land surveyors then withdrew -
So did Macdonald's Governor too.
Fort Garry was the new H.Q.
And over it a new flag flew -
The Métis flag for all to see,
Resplendent with the fleur de lis.

Riel proclaimed a government
And was elected President.
Macdonald sent out Donald Smith
For Louis' men to parley with:
His promises were just a myth.
The Métis, thinking they were meant,

Believed that Canada's intent
Was totally benevolent.

And so they set their prisoners free,
But they abused their liberty.
Each called himself a Canada Firster:
As racists, there was no one worster.
They marched in fury on Fort Garry
But snowdrifts forced the troops to tarry
And so the expedition failed:
They were surrounded, caught and jailed.

Perhaps unwisely then, Riel
Called on their leader in his cell.
He was a man called Thomas Scott,
The angriest bigot of the lot.

He threatened he would kill Riel -
He beat the warder up as well.
For bearing arms against the state
Scott went on trial and learned his fate:
By firing squad his end he'd make.
It proved to be a big mistake:
Scott's standing up to then was zero,
But now he was Ontario's hero.

Macdonald wished the Métis nation
To join the growing Federation
So with a Métis delegation
He did a deal for integration.

Riel's dream province was a fact
Under the Manitoba Act.
Riel rejoiced, but in the end
Found John Macdonald was no friend.

The velvet glove, he'd understand,
Concealed a ruthless iron hand.
The force that claimed it came to police
Would never give the rebels peace.

And so Riel was forced to roam,
An exile from his own true home.
And though three times his people sent
Riel to sit in Parliament
The Government despite this call
Would not admit him there at all.
At last, "You're pardoned," they would say,
"Provided that you stay away."

The Métis, overwhelmed and fleeced
By settlers coming from the east,
By now had in large numbers gone
To live by the Saskatchewan.
From tribal ancestors they came,
And felt the land was theirs to claim.

Though Ottawa at length agreed,
It acted with such lack of speed
The Métis knew they must rebel -
And who could lead them but Riel?

And Louis welcomed the decision -
He had a messianic vision
That he was chosen now to be
The man to make his people free.

With meetings and a Bill of Rights
He tried to do it with no fights.
But secret forces then were sent
By John Macdonald's government
Which feared the Métis, wanting more,
Would spark a greater Civil War.

Only two Cree lent their might
To give support to Louis' fight.
And yet he found that he could meet
The soldiers, and inflict defeat.

Louis Riel's success in arms
Set off a series of alarms -
Macdonald said in some despair:
"We need to get troops quickly there."

The railroad's chief said, "We will chance it
If you in turn will just finance it!"
So, soon the railroad's gaps were filled,
The troops sent, many Métis killed -
Reduced, when ammunition fails,
To firing buttons, stones and nails.

The troops could no more be defied:
Riel surrendered and was tried.
He told the jury that his aim
Had always only been to claim
The land rights in his people's name:
But then the Guilty verdict came.

The jury made a plea for mercy:
The Crown, ignoring controversy,
Hanged Louis - and by that ensured
A quarrel that has still endured.
Rebel or martyr? Though he's gone,
The argument still carries on.

Riel declared it made him sick
That Protestant and Catholic
Could not shake hands - he voiced his fears
That this could take two hundred years.

Progress has since been somewhat slow -
Still, there's a century to go!

WILLIAM CORNELIUS VAN HORNE
(1843- 1915)

(Van Horne was a genius of the railroad, and when he became general manager of the Canadian Pacific in 1882, his powerful personality and organizing skills were able to get the coast-to-coast railway completed in record time.)

In 1843 was born
William Cornelius Van Horne.
At just fourteen, the bright young boy
Got railroad work in Illinois,
Rose in the ranks, and shortly knew
Each railroad job there was to do.

Canadians said, "Now here's a star:
We'll let him run the C.P.R.!"
And so Van Horne began with zest
To build a railroad to the West.

In Winnipeg he made his base:
It was a booming, bustling place
Where real estate's great fluctuation
Depended on the speculation:
"Where will they put the railroad station?"

This happened all along the line
As people hankered for a sign
Of where the stops would be located -
For there the prices escalated.

Whole towns grew up, and their position
Depended on Van Horne's decision.

In the Canadian Pacific
Some thought him great, and some horrific.
His nickname had a certain sting:
They called him Boss of Everything -
And anyone who answered back
Was sure to find he'd got the sack.
Indeed he ruled the C.P.R.
Just like a fierce, despotic Czar.

And yet in most of those he hired
A fervent loyalty he inspired.
Using his methods, crews could lay
Up to four miles of track a day,
And he himself went out and back
To check the current End of Track.

When on these trips he often might
Play poker with the men all night
And then, such were his staying powers
Van Horne would work for fourteen hours.

To everybody's admiration
He still had time for recreation -
Collected fossils, drew cartoons
And on his violin played tunes;
Practical jokes he liked to do,
And he was fond of gardening too.

Asked where his powers had their source
He said, "From food and drink of course.
I eat and drink all that I can
And smoke as much as any man!"

The rails pushed on across the prairie
And made the tribes who roamed there wary.
They saw their hunting grounds cut back
By settlements along the track.

The Rockies shortly would be reached
But where would that stark range be breached?
Van Horne chose a disputed course:
He'd use the Pass at Kicking Horse.

Some said he never could complete
That dangerous and daring feat.
Thousands upon those peaks did swarm
Confronting avalanche and storm,
Dangled by ropes to cut and hack
The dizzy ledge to hold the track.
Rocks blasted out by dynamite
Sped forth like cannon-balls in flight.
Men tumbled from the precipice
And fell into the deep abyss.
Tall bridges, out of timber made,
Across the canyons swung and swayed.

In squalid camps the men survived
While secret whisky peddlers thrived.

The stuff was cutely smuggled in
Sometimes in bibles made of tin,
In eggs, and loco boilers too -
And once an organ held the brew.

Van Horne would come to see the work:
There was no danger he would shirk.
Walking for miles, great risks he'd take,
And fell once in an icy lake.

And all the while, he took great chances
To save the C.P.R.'s finances,
Put his own money in the stock
And claimed it was as firm as rock.
And when things got into a fix
He even played at politics,
Supplying a luxurious train
To help supporters to campaign.

When Van Horne to the west coast came
He chose Vancouver's site, and name.
Back east his powers still didn't lapse:
Somehow he filled the final gaps.
For years he'd kept the plans alive,
And got them done in less than five.

And now, as highest praise was given,
The very Last Spike could be driven.
At Craigellachie, in B.C.,
There gathered many a V.I.P.,

And happily they cheered and clamoured
To see, at last, the Last Spike hammered.

Van Horne, who must have felt relief
As well as pride, was very brief:
"Now this is all that I can say:
The work's well done in every way."
The bearded and top-hatted crowd
All cheered and clapped him long and loud.

Van Horne's amazing operation
Had forged the rails that spanned a nation.
He'd built two thousand miles of track,
And yet Van Horne could not sit back.
A quarter century he spent
As chairman and as president
Ensuring people near and far
Knew all about the C.P.R.

The whole rail network, out of pride,
Stopped for five minutes when he died,
So that all Canada could mourn
William Cornelius Van Horne.

12-LOUIS CYR
(1863 - 1912)

(French Canadian Louis Cyr defeated all challengers to be hailed as the strongest man in the world, a title he would probably still have if he were around today.)

Louis at birth the world astounds:
He weighs no less than eighteen pounds.
His father said, "I think we ought
To reinforce the baby's cot."

The beefy, blond and burly boy
Became his mother's pride and joy.
With curling tongs she curled his hair,
But no one dared to point or stare;
For Louis was, though groomed and curled,
The strongest man in all the world.

When just eighteen, he showed his force
By lifting up a full-grown horse.
One girl who watched him said, "I fear
I've lost my heart to Louis Cyr."
Melina Comtois was elated
To find her love reciprocated.

They married, but a former beau
Called David, loth to let her go,
Thought Louis' triumph he would check
By challenging him, in Quebec.

They chose a field all strewn with boulders
And tried to lift them on their shoulders.
They matched each other, rock by rock,
But one last boulder brought a shock.

Though David wrenched and strained to lift it
He found he simply couldn't shift it.
But Louis, as the cheers rang round,
Lifted that rock right off the ground.

Then later, Louis got the call
To join the police in Montreal.
When thugs attacked him in the street
He'd simply lift them off their feet.
Three men at once, on one occasion,
He carried thus into the station.

He toured in England where, amazed,
Crowds gasped to see the weights he raised.
Five hundred pounds he lifted there
With just one finger, in the air.
And quite as marvellous a feat
Was what the champion could eat.
He'd nonchalantly put away
Some twenty pounds of meat a day.

Back home, soon eighteen men he sat
Upon a plank - all very fat.
Without a groan, upon his back
He lifted up that paunchy pack.

They weighed four thousand pounds and more:
No strong man since has reached that score.

So let us honour, if you please,
This great Canadian Hercules.

MAY IRWIN
(1863-1938)

(May Irwin was the stage name of May Campbell, who began her theatre career in her teens and was soon an international star. In the 1890's she caused a sensation when she featured in the first kiss ever seen on the cinema screen.)

Mrs Campbell, best of mothers,
Like Mrs Worthington and others
Decided at a tender age
To put her daughters on the stage.

But Whitby in Ontario
Was not the place to make a show,
So Mrs Campbell thought she'd go
Across the lake to Buffalo.

The "Irwin Sisters" got the chance
To demonstrate their song and dance.
The show's producer was impressed -
Which proves that Mother knows what's best.
And soon the pair, so pert and pretty,
Became the toast of New York City.

Now even by the age of twenty
May Irwin had accomplished plenty.
She branched out in her stage career
And as an actress did appear.
Her theatre reputation grew
In London and in Paris too.

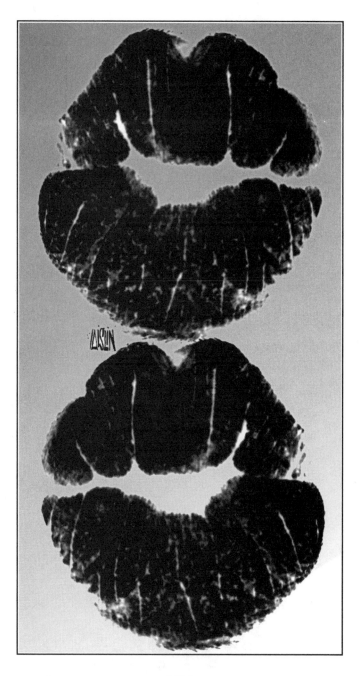

But stage success and foreign trips
Though glamorous, could not eclipse
The fame that came to her two lips.

For Thomas Edison, the man
With whom the movies first began,
Had got a plan that could not miss:
The filming of the first Screen Kiss.

In those first Motion Picture days
Short, flickering features were the craze
And trains filmed entering a station
Would cause an audience sensation.

Five days of filming were required,
Which made the kissers very tired
But got what Edison desired:
The cinemas were choc-a-bloc
As audiences gasped with shock
And moralists declared with gravity
The film would lead to gross depravity.

Just one more film was made by May
For she preferred the Great White Way,
And every time that she appeared
The audiences clapped and cheered.

She made a fortune, with panache,
And with investments shrewd, not rash,
Survived unscathed the Wall Street crash.

May on the Thousand Islands made
A home where Glitterati stayed
And six grand pianos could be played.

At one of these, one idle day
Irving Berlin sat down to play
And with a flourish of his hand
Wrote Alexander's Ragtime Band.

May had produced, her fans to please,
Records, and books of recipes,
And in her sixties she could still
In any theatre, top the bill.

Flamboyant as the life she led,
May ordered that, when she was dead,
She should be buried, dressed in red.

JACK MINER
(1865-1944)

(Jack Miner was a hunter who turned conservationist. He established one of the very first bird sanctuaries, at Kingsville in Ontario, and pioneered the charting of bird migration patterns.)

No one has had ideals much finer
Than ornithologist Jack Miner.
Indeed it's true, in other words,
His work was strictly for the birds.

Yet wild life and its conservation
Were not at first his occupation.
In youth the game, each time he'd spot it,
He simply raised his gun and shot it.

In Kingsville as a teenage boy
His hunting skills he would employ.
Barefoot he'd go through wood and field
To see what kind of prey they'd yield.
A dead skunk was, he used to think,
At fifty cents well worth the stink.

Jack and his brother Ted could make
A fee for every rattlesnake.
When grouse became their chosen prey
They'd bring back twenty in a day.
They slaughtered deer and duck and moose
And learned to honk just like a goose.

When Ted was accidentally killed
Jack's heart with anguished grief was filled.
The consolation which he sought
Was found in church, and there he taught
With acclamation as a rule,
A boys' class in the Sunday School.
They found his stories most exciting
And they helped him to master writing.

Quite soon he changed his attitude
To creatures he had once pursued.
He felt that they were more deserving
Of careful study and preserving.

He dug out ponds that geese would need
And planted trees and scattered seed,

Hoping the birds would understand
That here it would be safe to land.

The neighbours thought him somewhat weird,
Especially when no geese appeared.
It took four years till they'd begin
At last, to come and settle in.

Word must have spread, in Wild Goose Speak,
Passed eagerly from beak to beak,
That Kingsville was the place to seek.
And then it wasn't very long
Before each year the feathered throng
Was over fifty thousand strong.

His Sanctuary established, Jack
Thought their migration he would track.
He took a mallard and he put
A metal band around its foot;
Upon it his address was placed
So that the duck's flight could be traced.
Hundreds of miles south when it died,
Jack Miner soon was notified.

Thousands of birds each year were banded
So he'd discover where they landed.
Jack charted through this information
The wildfowls' pattern of migration.

Upon each band he also wrote
A short, uplifting Bible quote.
Who knows how many quick conversions
Resulted from those birds' excursions?

Jack toured and lectured and became
A famous conservation name.
Now Wildlife Week and his Foundation
Are part of his commemoration.
At Kingsville too the honking ranks
Of geese and ducks all voice their thanks!

MARTHA LOUISE BLACK
(1866-1957)

*(Martha Louise Black grew up in Chicago high society, but joined
the Klondike Gold Rush and went on to become 'Queen of the Yukon'
and only the second woman to sit in Canada's Parliament.)*

Martha, since she was a girl,
Had loved Chicago's social whirl.
But in her thirties she set forth
To journey to the frozen north.

Her two sons with her parents stayed.
Her husband other plans had made:
He didn't want to stay around
And soon he was Hawaii-bound.
But his departure didn't grieve her
For Martha had the Gold Rush fever.

A boat to Skagway called Utopia
Led to a golden cornucopia -
Or so she hoped as, climbing higher
Dressed in Victorian attire
Consistent with her social class
She scaled the fearsome Chilkoot Pass.
Then through the rapids she must go
To Dawson City down below.

She staked some claims but didn't find
The riches that she had in mind.

So on the seamy side of town
In "Lousetown" Martha settled down.

Some very hard times there she knew -
Then found that she was pregnant too.
Her neighbours helped - at last with joy
They greeted Martha's baby boy.
Typhoid, a fire, a landslide fall -
Mother and child survived them all.

Chicago now had lost its lure -
The Yukon was her home for sure.
She loved its majesty - for hours
She roamed to seek its plants and flowers.
And having energy to spare
She started up a sawmill there.

She wed a lawyer called George Black.
Ambitious plans he did not lack,
And soon they came to fine fruition
When George attained a high position.
As Top Man he could take a bow:
Commissioner of the Yukon now.

A long way from the Town called Louse,
Now Martha moved to Government House,
And very soon there she was gaining
Great fame for lavish entertaining
As well as growing there to boot,
Her vegetables, flowers and fruit.

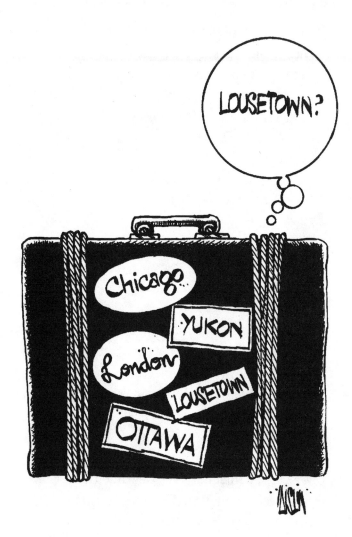

So celebrated had she grown,
As Lady Sourdough she was known.
To those who liked a regal name,
Queen of the Yukon she became.

When war came, George went off to France;
In London Martha took the chance
To publicize the Yukon there -
And she was honoured for her flair
In studying each flower variety
By the Royal Geographical Society.

Back home, George Black became M.P.
For Yukon's vast constituency.
When he was very ill, she said,
"I'll campaign for the seat instead!"
Around the territory she trekked
Saying, "I'm the one you should elect."

And that's how Martha came to be
At seventy, a new M.P. -
The second woman who was sent
To Ottawa and Parliament.
There Martha joined Agnes Macphail,
The only two who were not male.

And after that career she planned
A book on her beloved land.
She buckled down and got it done -
And lived till she was ninety-one.

AGNES MACPHAIL
(1890-1954)

(In 1921 Agnes Macphail became the first woman MP elected to Canada's House of Commons. She braved derision and hostility to champion the causes she believed in.)

Women voted since 1918
But no woman MP there had been
    Until Agnes Macphail
    Startled many a male
By invading the Ottawa scene.

She scorned male cabals and Old Pallery
And was mocked by the Press in the gallery.
    They all thought her bats,
    For she wouldn't wear hats
And suggested MPs cut their salary!

She withstood all the glares and the jeers
And stayed there for near twenty years.
    She campaigned for Disarmers
    And miners and farmers,
Till at last all the jeers turned to cheers.

EMILY CARR
(1871-1945)

(Emily Carr, one of Canada's greatest and most original painters, had to wait till she was fifty before her art got any wide recognition. She grew up in Victoria, not the ideal setting for her eccentric and volatile personality. But her great joy was travelling among the distant forest and coastal communities of British Columbia, whose lifestyle and totem pole art she recorded in her work.)

The Old World painters were inclined
To think that Art should be refined.
Canada's landscape they pooh-poohed:
"Those vistas are too vast and crude -
Unpaintable, that's what they are!"
But then, along came Emily Carr.

Her early sketches go right back
To charcoal portraits, on a sack.
Another childhood interest grew
In cherishing wild creatures too.
She tamed a squirrel and a crow -
And played guitar, and learned to sew.

In that strict family of nine
She was most often out of line,
And she remained throughout her life
A rebel who attracted strife.

Into the forest she would roam,
The local people's ancient home;

And so began her fascination
For many a centuries-old First Nation.

Some of the early friends she made
Lived near a Mission where she stayed.
Liking her warmth and sense of fun
They called her Klee Wyck - 'Laughing One'.
(The Mission, treated with aversion
By contrast, made just one conversion.)

In England then she studied art;
A suitor who had lost his heart
Followed her there across the sea
And kept on asking, "Marry me!"

This happened several times a week,
And she'd refuse each time he'd speak.
In fact, though several suitors tried,
She never did become a bride.

Back home, Victoria's ways she mocked:
Her sisters were extremely shocked.
She smoked, her words were sometimes coarse -
She even rode astride a horse!

Vancouver made a change of scene:
There, happier than she'd ever been,
She taught enthusiastically
Surrounded by her 'family' -
A dog, raccoons, a cockatoo,

Squirrels and chipmunks formed the crew.
Students, in spite of all these creatures,
Found Emily the best of teachers.

The places that she loved the most
Were in the woods and on the coast.
She got to know the vital roles
Played by the huge, carved totem poles.
She painted pictures of them, fearing
This art would soon be disappearing.

On Emily's journeys with her tent
A small menagerie always went.
The dog and cockatoo both came -
Even a vulture she'd made tame.

The villages and woods inspired her
And then a trip to Paris fired her:
She saw, instead of old precision,
A new art with a big, bold vision.
Now Emily with this art acquainted,
Knew how her landscape could be painted.

But back at home, her striking style
Provoked a condescending smile.
They called the work of Emily Carr
Childish and clumsy and bizarre.
Her sister, blind to Emily's aims,
Told her, "I simply love the frames!"

She kept on painting, loving best
The coast and forests of the West.
Their people's outlook she could share,
And found her firmest friendships there.

But even artists have to eat,
And Emily, to make ends meet,
Ran an apartment house, although
The dining-room made quite a show -
It doubled as a studio.
She felt this life was like a penance
And used to fight with all the tenants.

No fame or fanfares Emily knew
Till she was over fifty-two.
The National Gallery played a part:
It staged a show of West Coast Art.
At that exciting exhibition
Her art at last got recognition.

She'd been praised long ago in Paris:
Now she delighted Lawren Harris.
Soon she attained artistic heaven -
A show among the Group of Seven.
In Lawren Harris she had found
A mentor, fiery and profound.

He bought her paintings and declared:
"This Western genius must be shared.
If for a masterpiece you search,

Here's Emily's painting, Indian Church".

So Emily Carr at last became
In art a celebrated name;
And when she reached her seventieth year
Began a literary career.

Her stories brought her instant fame:
The first book's title was the same
As that fine nickname she had won -
Klee Wyck, which means The Laughing One.

LORD BEAVERBROOK
(1879-1964)

(Lord Beaverbrook was born Max Aitken and grew up in New Brunswick. He showed an early talent for making money especially by company mergers, and when he went to England he used his wealth to become a newspaper tycoon, and his personality to make his mark among the top politicians of his time.)

Max Aitken's earliest experience
Was spent among the Presbyterians;
But though his father was a preacher
Morals weren't Max's greatest feature.
His raffish youth, though, did reveal
His tendency to wheel and deal.

By eighteen, he'd been seen to dally
With frozen meats, a bowling alley,
The law and the insurance trade -
And then the mergers game he played.

Small companies gave Max the urge
To buy them up and then to merge,
And by these slick amalgamations
To fashion giant corporations.

In property, cement and steel,
Max took the plunge and did the deal.
He sidestepped any legal hitches
And made himself enormous riches.

So off to England then he went
And soon got into Parliament.
Fellow-Canadian Bonar Law
Max Aitken's great potential saw
And helped his progress, for he knew
That he was from New Brunswick too.

  Max got political rewards:
A peerage in the House of Lords.
He wondered then what name would seem
To suit him, and recalled a stream
Where as a child he used to look
At beavers swimming - so he took
The name of Baron Beaverbrook.

As well as being a Lord he soon
Became a newspaper tycoon.
He craved the power and the success
He thought would come with the Express.

He was a brash, hands-on proprietor -
His staff all wished that he was quieter,
But they endured the barking tone
That roared instructions down the phone.

Luxuriously the Beaver sat
In country house or London flat,
French villa, or on faraway
Verandahs in Montego Bay,
And like some medieval Czar

Controlled his lackeys from afar.

At Max's orders they'd crusade
For policies like Empire Trade.
While Hitler's threats grew more and more
And Europe knew what lay in store
Lord Beaverbrook's three papers bore
The headline, THERE WILL BE NO WAR!

When war came, Beaverbrook would get
A place in Churchill's Cabinet -
For Churchill was just one great name
Whose friendship Beaverbrook could claim.
His magnetism would delight
The politicians, left and right:
Nye Bevan, Michael Foot, Lloyd George -
Strong bonds with all of them he'd forge.

At dinner in his country house
The great and famous would carouse;
But first for cocktails, Max would fix
The daiquiris he loved to mix.

In politics, his guests all knew
He was a powerful fixer too -
And how he loved to stir the brew!
His wealth and contacts gave the means
To wheel and deal behind the scenes,
And secretly he'd interfere
With many a promising career.

In machinations and intrigues
Old Max was in the Major Leagues.
No wonder that, while many fêted him
A lot of others really hated him.

By Churchill's wife he was abused:
"A microbe!" was the term she used.
He had vendettas, tried to flatten
The reputation of Mountbatten,
Detested Baldwin, growled and glowered
If someone mentioned Noel Coward.

Yet all the schemes he liked to cherish
Were mostly doomed to fail and perish.
He'd tell his papers: "Rant and rage,
And put my views on every page!
The public then will quickly gauge
Just what the only way to vote is."
The public simply took no notice!

One of his editorial crew
Remarked when he was feeling blue:
"In Fleet Street, one great fact is true -
Experience to me has taught it:
No cause is lost, till we support it!"

Lord Beaverbrook, forever proud
Of his home province, there endowed
Town halls and squares and rinks for skaters,
Organs and steeples and theaters.

There, almost everywhere you look
You find the name of Beaverbrook.

As H.G.Wells was wont to say:
"Perhaps his soul's alive today
Making, before the final knell,
A merger between Heaven and Hell!"

ELIZABETH ARDEN
(1882-1966)

(Elizabeth Arden was born Florence Nightingale Graham, in Ontario. Believing that 'women have the right to be beautiful', she set about helping them with treatments and cosmetics that brought her world-wide fame and fortune.)

This fact not many people know:
Elizabeth Arden's name was Flo.
Woodbridge Ontario was the site
Where little Flo first saw the light.
The Grahams' baby didn't wail
When christened Florence Nightingale,
But that was quite a mouthful, so
She quickly shortened it to Flo.

She did try nursing, but was sure
Rather than medicines to cure
She would prefer to make and sell
Products to beautify the well.

So to the kitchen then she went
Determined to experiment.
The stench resulting from her labours
Asphyxiated all the neighbours.

But Flo, in spite of their vexation,
Knew she had found her true vocation,
And though her father went berserk,
Off to New York she went to work.

And there a new career begins:
Tight straps pull in the clients' chins
While expert hands massage the faces
And cream smooths out Time's tell-tale traces.
This, Beauty Parlours tell their clients,
Is not just pampering, but Science.

Ladies once thought it would deprave you
Improving on what Nature gave you,
But what once smacked of impropriety
Was now the rage in High Society.

Soon Flo fulfilled her bold intent
To start her own establishment.
She teamed up with Elizabeth Hubbard
Who'd many potions in her cupboard,
And with Flo's skills and selling flair
They seemed to be the perfect pair.

But Flo's hot temper led to strife
Which happened often in her life.
Flo on her own then staked her claim
But kept Elizabeth's first name.
The Arden which she added on
Came from a work by Tennyson.

Her salon in Fifth Avenue
Into a massive empire grew.
At first when times were rather lean
She got there first, to sweep and clean.

The salon, though, was made luxurious
And there she reigned, petite and furious.
She sacked employees by the score;
 One girl said, "Working there is more
Like being in a revolving door."

But before long demand was huge
For Arden face powders and rouge,
Mascaras, cleansing creams, and oceans
Of tonics, muscle oils and lotions,
All claiming that they'd bring perfection
To every customer's complexion.

Elizabeth had tried herself
Each product that was on the shelf.
She practiced, such was her persistence,
Many times too on her assistants.

As well as a persuasive title
She knew that packaging was vital
And used her fine designing skills
On ribbons, furbelows and frills.

In spite of its refined appeal
The Beauty Game was not genteel:
Elizabeth had nerves of steel
And battled all along the line
With her great rival, Rubenstein.

They never met and never spoke,
Treating each other as a joke.
The rival's name was never said:
"That woman" was the term instead.

She took up yoga and devised
A room where clients exercised,
And made, with outcome most rewarding,
The world's first exercise recording.

And then in Maine, for something new,
She pioneered the Health Spa too.
Among the treatments she would deem
Essential to the day's regime
Were headstands, Youth Masks for the skin
And also baths in paraffin.

Soon as a hobby she was able
To buy herself a racehorse stable.
She painted it pink, white and blue,
And even had piped music too.
In baby-talk she'd bill and coo
To stop her "darlings" feeling blue.

Though jockeys chuckled at her notions
They rubbed the horses with her lotion.
Thanks maybe to these airs and graces
Her horses won a lot of races.

She married twice, had two divorces,
But stayed devoted to her horses.
At eighty, still alert and keen
She ruled her empire like a queen.

Thousands whom she'd beautified
Turned out to mourn her when she died.
One woman found the strange thought strike her:
"Miss Arden dead? That's so unlike her!"

JOSEPH-ARMAND BOMBARDIER
(1908-1964)

(From his teenage years Bombardier showed his creative skill with machinery, and went on to invent the snowmobile and the ski-doo, and to found the internationally successful company that still bears his name.)

All through his childhood and his teens
Bombardier just loved machines.
While other less ingenious boys
Were playing ball or breaking toys
Young Armand's interest was greater
In fiddling with the carburator.
He thought kids' games were just for mugs -
He'd rather clean the sparking plugs.

His father, thinking him a star,
Said, "What a clever lad you are!
So here's an ancient car, my son -
Dismantling it could be fun."

So Armand, grateful to his dad,
Embarked on an idea he had.
He planned a vehicle to go
With passengers, across the snow.

He took the engine out, and fit
Four ski-like runners under it.
Then, being a most inventive feller,
He built himself a large propeller.

With this he would, such was his plan,
Replace the radiator fan.

"Allons, mon petit frère!" he told
His younger brother, Léopold.
Said Armand, "I'll be on the back
To keep the vehicle on track
While at the front end, brother dear,
You sit and use your feet to steer."

Then after each took up his perch
The strange device began to lurch
And judder forward, slowly sliding,
The brothers perilously riding.

Along the snowbound streets they went
Creating great astonishment.
The folk of Valcourt in Quebec
Thought one at least would break his neck.

They zigged and zagged from side to side
While gleefully young Armand cried:
"I had a dream and made it real,
And here it is - the Snowmobile!"

Knowing his genius was large
His father built him a garage
And here with purpose unrelenting
Bombardier went on inventing -

Learned English too, so he could read
The science journals he would need.

The Snowmobile he engineered
Had tracks, and skis in front that steered.
He toured Quebec to flaunt its glories
And featured much in front-page stories.

It met with widespread admiration,
Transforming winter transportation.
Doctors and priests and rescue crews,
The postal service bearing news
And many more, found great appeal
In Armand's wondrous Snowmobile.

Then he devised a new machine:
The Ski-Doo zoomed upon the scene.
A zippy, zappy new sensation,
A must for winter recreation.

His company went on to do
Trains, aeronautics, sea-doos too -
And, honouring Bombardier's fame
The company still bears his name.

Yet no advance in transportation
Could match the wild exhilaration
Of that first journey through the snow
One day in Valcourt, long ago.

WINNIE THE POOH

*(The origins of A.A.Milne's famous character can be traced back to
a Canadian bear cub which became a First World War army mascot.)*

The Second Infantry Brigade
By train a wartime journey made:
White River in Ontario
Was on the route they had to go,
And Captain Colebourn spotted there
A most enchanting baby bear.

The Captain promptly thought he'd get
The little black cub as a pet.
He said, "I'll mark my home town's fame
By making Winnipeg its name."

Soon known as Winnie, she was made
The mascot of the whole brigade.
In England where they went to train
They had a camp on Salisbury Plain.
Winnie was petted, praised and fed,
And slept beneath the Captain's bed.

But when the troops went off to war
Winnie could stay with him no more.
The Zoo was asked, for the duration,
To give the bear accommodation.

Soon, capering around her cage
Winnie the bear was all the rage.
She'd roll around and wave her paws
And revel in the crowd's applause.

The Captain, when the war had ended,
Thought Winnie's winning ways were splendid.
It would be best for her, he knew,
To leave her there in London Zoo.

The children loved her - there was one
Called Christopher, A.A.Milne's young son,
Who at the age of five or six
Was just delighted with her tricks.

His father wrote, to please the boy,
A tale that children would enjoy
In which a teddy bear did feature;
Winnie was what he called the creature,
After the bear in London Zoo
And so was born Winnie the Pooh.

The real bear died in quiet old age -
Her namesake though still holds the stage,
Alive and kicking on the page.

White River in commemoration
Now holds an annual celebration
To honour Captain Colebourn's name
And that young cub who rose to fame:

Winnie, the bear who gained such glory
By starring in a children's story.

JOE SHUSTER
(1914-1992)

(Toronto-born Joe Shuster was the artist who created that famous comic-book and screen hero, Superman, still going strong after sixty years.)

When Joe Shuster was a boy
Drawing was his greatest joy.
In Joe's young, fertile mind began
That great creation, SUPERMAN.

With words dreamed up by Jerry Siegal,
The Man of Steel swooped like an eagle
And soon became the scourge of crooks
And hero of the comic books.
He still remained in all his tussles
A man of modesty - and muscles.

It's always said Toronto is
The model for Metropolis;
Toronto's Star too, if you scan it,
Could have inspired the Daily Planet.
As for Clark Kent, those in the know
Declare that he resembled Joe.

Perhaps Joe, spectacled and shy,
Wished that he too could zoom and fly,
And thought that it would just be bliss
To make that metamorphosis.

What joy to quickly change your shape
And don blue tights and scarlet cape,
An S emblazoned on your chest
So people know that you're the best,
And will defeat the villains now
With many a WHAM! and SPLAT! and POW!
(A phone booth, though, does seem a strange
And rather awkward place to change.)

The hero and his letter S
Became an overnight success.
Was it a bird? Was it a plane?
And did Clark Kent love Lois Lane?

His hectic role in fighting crime
Left him, of course, so little time -
But they were quite a daunting team,
Frustrating many a deadly scheme:
Those Monsters, Androids, Things from Space -
They quickly put them in their place.

His hero's fame became substantial
But Joe's reward was not financial.
A hundred dollars, that was what
Brave Superman's creator got.
The publishers, to their delight,
Had bought the total copyright.

Later, when Joe and Jerry Siegal
Maintained the deal had not been legal

And sued to get their hero back
They lost the case, and got the sack.

If only then the x-ray eyes
Of Superman, alert and wise,
Could have observed their misery,
And crying, "Here's a job for me!"
Their hero could have taken flight
And come and seized their copyright!
Sadly, that kind of noble act
Happens in fiction, not in fact.

And now, though his creator's gone
The Man of Steel still carries on.
Although he's over sixty now
He still can WHAM! and ZAP! and POW!
Delighting every ardent fan
Of young Joe Shuster's SUPERMAN.

JAY SILVERHEELS
(1919-1980)

(Jay Silverheels grew up on the Six Nations Reserve at Brantford, Ontario, where he triumphed in many different sports. He went to Hollywood with a Canadian All-Stars lacrosse team, and stayed there to become a screen star, especially known for his role as Tonto in "The Lone Ranger".)

Jay Silverheels, born Harold Smith,
Became a name to conjure with.

A Mohawk whose athletic verve
Made him the star of his Reserve,
He triumphed both on track and field.
Crowds cheered him and opponents reeled
To see the power that he could wield.

His grandfather, a Mohawk chief,
Declared his skills beyond belief
And said, "Henceforth I do decree
Your name Jay Silverheels shall be."

Young Jay was never at a loss
In hockey, boxing or lacrosse.
At twenty he fulfilled a dream
And toured with a Canadian team,
And their lacrosse was just so good
They were the toast of Hollywood.

There the comedian Joe E. Brown
Persuaded Jay to settle down;
He said, "The claim I want to prove is
That I can get you into movies!"

He did just that, but at the start
Jay only got a walk-on part.
Though he was diligent and dextrous,
`For years he stayed among the extras.

But then at last the breakthrough came:
The role of Tonto made his name.
The masked Lone Ranger could not ride
Without brave Tonto by his side.

His horse was Silver, and he said
"Hi-yo!" to that great quadruped.
To show he valued human life,
The Ranger, when confronting strife,
Had silver bullets which he used.
The victims must have been confused,
Remarking as they dropped down dead,
"At least the bullet wasn't lead!"

Silver's his theme, the Ranger feels:
For bullets, horse - and Silverheels.

Young audiences thronged to see
The Ranger ride to victory

As he and Tonto did their best
To bring true justice to the West.

In real life Jay helped when he could
Others who came to Hollywood,
And founded, his success to share,
The Indian Actors Workshop there.

Jay and his colleagues' work redressed
The image of the old Wild West
Where noble cowboys were dependable
And savage Indians expendable.

And when he died, they put his name
In Hollywood's big Walk of Fame
Where all the great performers are:
Beside Sinatra's, there's Jay's star -
An all-time tribute that reveals
The talent of Jay Silverheels.

BEATRICE LILLIE
(1898-1989)

(Beatrice Lillie began her performing career as a member of the Lillie Trio with her mother and sister in Toronto. She went on to become a comedienne who delighted audiences on both sides of the Atlantic, as well as such stars as Charlie Chaplin and Noel Coward.)

Bea said: "At twelve, I just stopped growing -
My nose, however, kept on going."
Although she felt her nose lacked charm
It sure did her career no harm.

Her marvelously mobile face
Could make them laugh with one grimace.
From slapstick falls to caustic wit
Her style made Bea a world-wide hit.
They called her, with those beads she twirled,
The funniest woman in the world.

But as a girl, a taste she had
For ballads serious and sad.
The one she really used to love
Was Oh, for the wings, for the wings of a dove.

Her mother and her sister made
The Lillie Trio, and they played
And entertained, with great propriety,
Toronto's most genteel society.

Beatrice Lillie and Jimmy Durante: Separated at birth?

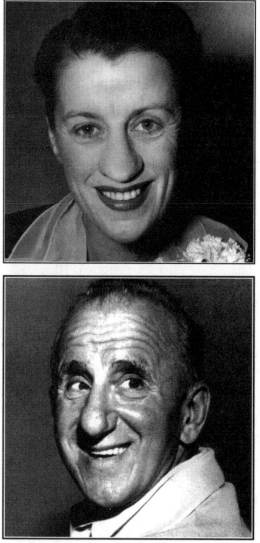

Bea always dreamed that she'd go far
And be a famous movie star;
She even planned her name as well -
She'd call herself Gladys Montell.

She went to movies all the time
Whenever she possessed a dime.
She little thought one day she'd sing
With Julie Andrews and with Bing.

At boarding school she had no chances
For any nice teenage romances:
Boys came in once a year, to dances.
Bea once led girls in crocodile
Into a bank, to give a smile
To one young teller she preferred -Then
marched them out, without a word.

And then the end of schooldays found
Young Beatrice Lillie London-bound.
The Lillie Trio were together
But disappointment Bea must weather.
She spent her days auditioning
Without achieving anything.
She sang "I hear you calling me" -
Producers, though, did not call Bea.

Then finally she got a call -
A solo spot in Music Hall.
They introduced her to the throng

As Canada's Sweetheart of Song.
The first song that she'd brought along
Was quite a weepie - or a gurgler! -
"Don't steal my prayer-book, Mr Burglar."

She finished, bowed - and to her ears
Came Cockney catcalls, boos and jeers.
Gritting her teeth she carried on
And in the next song, truly shone.
She introduced it with a grin
As "by my friend, Irving Berlin."
And then the audience that jeered her
Eventually stood and cheered her.

Her breakthrough came, the legend goes,
When one of André Charlot's shows
Auditioned singers - Bea was sure
That if she went there looking poor,
A battered suitcase in her hand,
They'd sympathize, and think her grand.

They didn't, till with style and grace
She bowed, and tripped upon the case.
She fell spreadeagled, looking daft -
And those producers, how they laughed!
And she and they perceived it then:
This girl was a comedienne!

And after that she didn't stop:
Quite soon she'd reach the very top.

In musicals and in revues
She made ecstatic headline news;
And then she made more headlines yet
By marrying a Baronet.

Now Beatrice Lillie, she'd reveal,
Was also known as Lady Peel.
Soon after, a Chicago crowd
Bowed back at her, when Beatrice bowed.

Now Beatrice Lillie was the toast
Of audiences coast to coast.
Toronto gave her accolades -
Met her with bands and big parades;
She captivated Europe too
In cabaret and in revue.

Now Charlie Chaplin said her art
Made her his female counterpart,
And Noel Coward wrote specially
Mad Dogs and Englishmen for Bea.

In Hollywood she found no thrill:
She'd rather be in Vaudeville.
At wartime troop shows she was feted
And by de Gaulle was decorated.

She starred in Thoroughly Modern Millie,
An Evening with Beatrice Lillie,

And then gained even greater fame
By playing the role of Auntie Mame.

Soon audiences for TV
Discovered the delights of Bea.
She had the longest of careers:
It lasted more than sixty years -
A sign of what her fans did feel
For Beatrice Lillie, Lady Peel.

OSCAR PETERSON
(Born 1925)

(Born in Montreal, Oscar Peterson was already playing in bands and on the radio when he was in his teens. With his flamboyant style and personality, he soon went on to achieve world-wide popularity and to play with, and be admired by, all the greatest jazz musicians.)

Oscar, as a virtuoso,
Made other pianists seem just so-so.
This boy who came to wow them all
From London to Carnegie Hall
Was born and raised in Montreal.

Oscar, like all the children, had
Good music lessons from his dad:
He was a porter by profession,
But music was his great obsession.
At school, young Oscar would astound
His fellow-students, gathered round
To hear his boogie-woogie sound.

He won at fourteen, easily,
A contest at the CBC
And soon in his own weekly show
Played piano on the radio.

He wanted to leave school to play;
His father let him have his way,
But said: "Son - be, unlike the rest,
Not just a player, but the Best!"

His father's words young Oscar heeded
And aiming for the top, succeeded.
He played with bands, made records too,
And soon his reputation grew.

Now Oscar got his greatest chance
When he was heard by Norman Granz.
The famous impresario
Declared: "I want you in my show.

Jazz at the Philharmonic's fame
Will very quickly make your name."
So at Carnegie Hall he played,
And what an impact there he made!
With Ray Brown on the double bass
He quite electrified the place.

From then on, his career was made -
In world-wide concert tours he played.
With Granz's troupe he would appear
In eighty cities in a year.

Crowds reveled at the expertise
Of this magician of the keys.
He seemed to play, his listeners reckoned,
At least a hundred notes a second.
One colleague said: "His pianos seem
So hot, they give off smoke and steam."

This suave and smiling, bear-like man
Was raved about by every fan.
The bracelet that he'd always wear -
A gift to him from Fred Astaire -
Dazzled, just like the watch he wore;
His music dazzled even more.

Practical jokes he played a lot
On colleagues, but revenge they got:
Stuck keys together, even hid
Steel balls inside the piano lid.

Arthritis plagued him, and he'd face
A lot of slurs upon his race.
In Canada he thought it bad
No black was in a TV ad;
Though that today seems very strange,
Oscar's campaign began the change.

At times some music critics panned him -
He said they couldn't understand him.
But though the critics might attack him,
His colleagues never failed to back him.

And Oscar played with all the greats
In Canada and in the States:
With Ella, Armstrong and Count Basie
And Dizzy, always acting crazy.
His various Trios reached the heights

Of challenge and of jazz delights.
Even Art Tatum was impressed
And Art, for Oscar, was the best.

As Oscar now recalls his story,
He ought to bask in all this glory.
A deluge of awards and praise
Honours the way that Oscar plays.

For as one music guru said
When asked: "Who would you like, when dead,
To be reincarnated as?" -
"I would be Oscar, King of Jazz!"

THE DIONNE QUINTS
(born 1934)

*(The Dionne Quints were the first identical quintuplets to sur-
vive. Their birth in a farmhouse at Callander, Ontario, caused a
worldwide sensation, and brought the family fame and fortune, and
many problems too.)*

The thought of giving birth to Quints
Would make a lot of mothers wince.
When Madame Dionne had her five
No-one believed they could survive.

For they were in a desperate plight:
No water or electric light
Was in the farmhouse where all night
Their mother laboured, giving birth
To this new wonder of the earth.

The doctor and the midwives strove
To warm the Quints before a stove.
A basket there was all they got
To make a cramped and crowded cot.
Their father felt a bit unsteady:
He'd seven children there already.

After a week, the weight they'd reach
Was little more than two pounds each.
And yet Annette and Emilie
Yvonne and Cécile and Marie

Survived to be a famous show
In Callander, Ontario,
And guaranteed the world would know
Of Doctor Allan Roy Dafoe.

For soon a gaggle of reporters
Was swarming round the Dionne daughters.
The newsreels whirred, the flashbulbs popped,
The hectic circus never stopped.
The doctor greeted with felicity
The massive media publicity.

Chicago's World Fair then reacted -
And soon they had Dionne contracted.
Off to the Fair the Quints would go,
Five little stars to steal the show.
But then the Government said "No!"

Ontario's rulers, quick to see
A golden opportunity,
Said, "For the Quints' sake, we declare
We're going to take them into care."

The Quints from home were quickly moved:
The public and the press approved.
They thought it only right - and so
Did Doctor Allan Roy Dafoe.

A hospital was soon erected
Just so the Quints could be protected.

They needed, in the doctor's view,
Protection from their parents too.
In theory they could come to call,
But were not welcomed there at all.
They tried to move in, feeling sore -
But very soon were shown the door.

And yet Dafoe, the Quints' physician,
Said they could go on exhibition.
Inside the hospital was made
A place where they could be displayed.
The children played there in their crèche;
Around the sides, a fine wire mesh
Screened off the eager public, who
Filed slowly past them, peering through.

To see the children, thousands came
To Quintland, as it soon became.
Their dresses must be all the same,
Which led psychologists to claim
Each had no individual role
But looked like guppies in a bowl.

Their guardians ignored such strictures
And put them into motion pictures;
And clearly they were perfect for
Endorsing products by the score.

Milk by Carnation, Oats by Quaker,
Even a disinfectant-maker,

Toothpaste and mattresses and soap
All found a new commercial scope
And soaring sales, upon the basis
Of those five small, cherubic faces.

The locals basked in all this glory:
In books the midwives sold their story.
In Mr Dionne's shop you'd find
Cheap souvenirs of every kind.
He also had a woolen shop,
While the garage where cars would stop
Had five pumps - yes, you get the hint -
Each named after a Dionne Quint.

Their father waged a big campaign
To get the children back again.
It took nine years though, to convince
The world that he should have the Quints.

At last opinion swung his way:
Public and press could now portray
The place made for the Quints to dwell
As very like a prison cell.

The guardians said that there should be
A new house for the family.
The parents then were quite delighted:
They and the Quints were reunited.

But there was little happiness:
Their freedom now was even less.
Their father never let them roam
Outside the fence around their home,
 And even kept two bears that growled
At any onlooker who prowled.
Their father, stern and quick to blame,
Still made the Quints all dress the same.

At eighteen they were sent away
To convent school at Nicolet.
Emilie died - her sisters, all
Grief-stricken, moved to Montreal;
And though their parents took it hard
The daughters sent no Christmas card.

Now trust fund arguments were rife
And legal battles dogged their life.
They said then, looking from a distance:
"Money, not love, ruled our existence."

Although such births are now not rare,
There've been no siblings anywhere
So famous, or unlucky, since
Ontario's five Dionne Quints.

JONI MITCHELL
(born 1943)

(Joni Mitchell grew up in Saskatoon where she first performed in coffee houses. Later in Toronto and then in Los Angeles her individual style and original songs made her a star on the performance circuit and on records.)

Joni was born in Fort MacLeod
And made her parents very proud.
She later said they'd counted on
A boy they'd christen Robert John,
But when the baby's sex was known
They changed it to Roberta Joan.

Some frugal times the family knew
In prairie towns where Joni grew.
She suffered a near-fatal blow
At nine years old, from polio;
But struggling bravely, she survived
And as a lithe teenager thrived.

She loved the party dancing scene,
Won contests as a Teenage Queen
And listened to rock music daily -
Then bought herself a ukulele.

Though modern styles did not come soon
To prairie towns like Saskatoon
Its coffee house, Louis Riel,
Was where the trendier types did well.

There Joni started her career;
Most liked her, although some would sneer.
At least she earned enough reward
To mean that now she could afford
 A real guitar, which all were thinking
Outclassed the ukulele's plinking.

And with this brand-new instrument
She started to experiment.
Eccentric tuning styles she made
To match whatever song she played,
And found her voice could quickly change
To span a most impressive range.

That range made Joni quite unique:
Like birds that glide from peak to peak
Ruling their kingdom in the sky
Her voice swooped low or soared up high.

"She sounds," one critic chose to grouse,
"Like someone swallowing a mouse!"
But many others found her voice
As classy as the best Rolls Royce.

Her toothy smile, her long blonde hair,
Made her distinctive everywhere.
In 1967 came
Her Chart success, The Circle Game.
Then with her reputation growing
She found she had the Urge for Going.

From town to town she made her way:
Toronto, New York, then L.A.
In Laurel Canyon there she stayed
And wrote the moving songs she played
And found she had a fortune made:
For writing songs and then recording
Had proved for Joni most rewarding.

She formed a lucrative creation,
Her own big music corporation;
And just to make the fortune swell
She purchased real estate as well.
She said, "I'm now, by some strange twist,
The only hippie capitalist!"
Relationships were less secure,
And restless Joni used to tour -
Guitar-case crammed with routes and maps
And lyrics scrawled on paper scraps.

Star rock groups Joni moved among
Like Crosby, Stills and Nash and Young -
Found love and lost it, went abroad
Where thousands gathered to applaud,
Spent time in Crete where hippie raves
Were held among the mountain caves.

But not all Joni's ways were wild -
Her life was often calm and mild:
She liked to cook and paint and knit,
Play cribbage when she'd time for it.

While as for fame, it waxed and waned.
Sometimes as Queen of Rock she reigned,
Her records reaching such success
Elvis himself was selling less.
Though sometimes too we must confess
She languished in the wilderness.

Now, Joni Mitchell's here to stay -
Grammy Awards have come her way
And most of all, her fans in throngs
Remember Joni's subtle songs:

Her poetry of love that ends,
Of hope and freedom, fickle friends,
Dreams of a river to skate away on,
Of Chelsea Mornings to greet the day on,
Of the paradise we haven't got,
Now paved to make a parking lot.
As one enamoured critic found:
"If angels sang, that's how they'd sound!"

OH, NO! MORE CANADIANS!

AUTHOR'S NOTE

Aislin and I found that when people said how much they enjoyed our first collection, *Oh! Canadians!* they often suggested other favorite characters they'd like to see given our treatment. There are so many spectacular, eccentric and courageous figures in Canada's past and present, that it would take volumes to cover them all. But we hope this second selection, like the first, will interest and entertain general readers, school students and history fans alike.

My research was much helped by the Canadian Embassy in Dublin and the London Library, and I am also grateful to Marsha Boulton for her entertaining biographies in *Just a Minute* and *Just Another Minute.*

Once again my great thanks and congratulations go to Aislin for another batch of superb illustrations, and to Kim McArthur for her constant help, enthusiasm and inspiration. We both wish her new publishing company the very best of success.

Gordon Snell